Challenge Club Passport

MFL – French

Name:

Class:

Teacher:

Published by JNPAQUET Books Ltd, LONDON.

Copyright © 2015 JNPAQUET Books Ltd.
All rights reserved.

A CIP catalogue record for this title is available from the British Library.

ISBN: 9781910909089
eISBN: 9781910909096

HOW DOES YOUR CHALLENGE CLUB PASSPORT WORK?

Attempt the challenges and receive rewards.

Ask your teacher to sign your challenge once it has been completed and include the work, or evidence, with your passport.

Use the *"CHALLENGE ME"* cards, located at the end of the passport, to acquire extra challenges or questions from your teacher.

Bonne chance!

Amy Sargent.

The Author of this
Challenge Club Passport
requests and requires all those
whom it may concern
to allow the bearer to take
the included challenges freely
without let or hindrance,
and to afford the bearer
such assistance with the work
as may be necessary.

Challenge 1

Speak.

In your lesson(s) this week, speak only French.

Date(s) Completed	Signed

How I felt about this challenge:

Challenge 2

Question.

Ask at least 10 questions in French, during your lesson.

Date(s) Completed	Signed

How I felt about this challenge:

Challenge 3

The Magazine.

Read a French magazine and then use the format to create your own magazine entry.

Date(s) Completed	Signed

How I felt about this challenge:

Challenge 4

Picture Word.

Take a word from a topic we have studied and create an image that both spells it and explains it.

Date(s) Completed	Signed

How I felt about this challenge:

Challenge 5

Joke.

Make up a joke, or a riddle, in French.
(Keep it clean, please!)

Date(s) Completed	Signed

How I felt about this challenge:

Challenge 6

The Film.

Independently watch a French film and review it. Think of a title for the sequel.

Date(s) Completed	Signed

How I felt about this challenge:

Challenge 7

Biography.

Research a famous French person and write a biography on them.

Date(s) Completed	Signed

How I felt about this challenge:

Challenge 8

Favourite Song.

Take the beat of your favourite song and replace the original words with French words. They could either be a translation or brand new words.

Date(s) Completed	Signed

How I felt about this challenge:

Challenge 9

Write to the PM.

The government have decided that languages no longer need to be learned. What would be the possible consequences if no-one studied languages? Write a letter to the Prime Minister to dissuade him.

Date(s) Completed	Signed

How I felt about this challenge:

Challenge 10

6 Steps.

Link a linguist to a mathematician in exactly six steps.

Date(s) Completed	Signed

How I felt about this challenge:

Challenge 11

The Exam Paper.

Create an exam paper that involves speaking, writing, reading and listening skills. You must also have a mark scheme and grade boundaries to accompany it.

Date(s) Completed	Signed

How I felt about this challenge:

Challenge 12

Jeopardy!

The answer is "languages". What are 5 possible questions.

Date(s) Completed	Signed

How I felt about this challenge:

Challenge 13

Another Language.

Learn numbers 1-10 and at least 5 basic greetings in another language (not including French or English!).

Date(s) Completed	Signed

How I felt about this challenge:

Challenge 14

The Song.

Listen to a French song (you can find many on *YouTube*) and note down as many words as you can recognise with their translations.

Date(s) Completed	Signed

How I felt about this challenge:

Challenge 15

Touring The World.

Invent a solution to the problems of communication that a singer, or a group, might face when touring the world.

Date(s) Completed	Signed

How I felt about this challenge:

Challenge 16

Favourites.

Translate your favourite TV shows or favourite films into French.

Date(s) Completed	Signed

How I felt about this challenge:

Challenge 17

The New Disney.

Create a new Disney hero, or villain. They have superpowers relating to MFL. What are they and how do they work? Explain in French. Also, label the features of your character, e.g. Their looks, personality, clothing, etc.

Date(s) Completed	Signed

How I felt about this challenge:

Challenge 18

Country Facts.

Research a French speaking country ar
write the facts in French. Rank them
order of importance.

Date(s) Completed	Signed

How I felt about this challenge:

Challenge 19

The Recipe.

Follow a French recipe (you can find these on *Google*) to make a delicious dish. Ask a family member to write a review on the dish. If you can't actually make the dish, translate the steps to English.

Date(s) Completed	Signed

How I felt about this challenge:

Challenge 20

The Review.

Read a short story in French and write a review. Would you have had the ending as it was or could you re-write it.

Date(s) Completed	Signed

How I felt about this challenge:

Challenge 21

The Arrest.

You have been arrested for not learning enough French words. Write a statement on why you are not guilty, using exactly 56 words.

Date(s) Completed	Signed

How I felt about this challenge:

Challenge 22

The Comic Strip.

Design and create a comic strip in French depicting the daily routine of your idol.

Date(s) Completed	Signed

How I felt about this challenge:

Challenge 23

Future.

How do you think learning French will change in the next 10 years? Consider the development of new technology and write a newspaper article with a gripping headline. Be sure to include advantages and disadvantages.

Date(s) Completed	Signed

How I felt about this challenge:

Challenge 24

The Statement.

Justify the following statement: Students should only study the core subjects of Maths, English and Science. Learning French should be removed from Education.

Date(s) Completed	Signed

How I felt about this challenge:

Challenge 25

The Novel.

Read a novel in French and write a review on it. How would you rate it and why? Before reading the ending, predict what will happen. Your school library may stock French books, if not, ask your teacher or, if you're lucky enough, you could buy one online. A good place to start might be *Le Petit Prince*.

Date(s) Completed	Signed

How I felt about this challenge:

Félicitations!

Congratulations on completing all 25 challenges! Ask your teacher to sign this page so you can receive your reward!

Date Passport was Completed	Signed

KEEP CALM
AND
CHALLENGE ME

KEEP CALM
AND
CHALLENGE ME

KEEP CALM
AND
CHALLENGE ME

KEEP CALM
AND
CHALLENGE ME

Printed in Great Britain
by Amazon.co.uk, Ltd.,
Marston Gate.